TEAM SPIRIT®

SMART BOOKS FOR YOUNG FANS

THE SAN ANTONIO SPURS

BY
MARK STEWART

NORWOOD HOUSE PRESS
CHICAGO, ILLINOIS

Norwood House Press
P.O. Box 316598
Chicago, Illinois 60631

For information regarding Norwood House Press, please visit our website at:
www.norwoodhousepress.com or call 866-565-2900.

All photos courtesy of Associated Press except the following:
Author's Collection (6), Topps, Inc. (15, 34 left, 38, 42 both), Fleer Corp. (21),
Black Book Partners (22, 37, 43 left), Sports Illustrated for Kids (23), SkyBox International (28),
San Antonio Spurs (33, 45), Beckett Publications, Inc. (34 right), San Antonio for Kids (36).
Cover Photo: John Raoux/Associated Press

The memorabilia and artifacts pictured in this book are presented for educational and informational purposes,
and come from the collection of the author.

Editor: Mike Kennedy
Designer: Ron Jaffe
Project Management: Black Book Partners, LLC.
Special thanks to Topps, Inc.

Library of Congress Cataloging-in-Publication Data

Stewart, Mark, 1960 July 7-
  The San Antonio Spurs / by Mark Stewart. -- Revised edition.
    pages cm. -- (Team spirit)
  Includes bibliographical references and index.
  Summary: "A revised Team Spirit Basketball edition featuring the San
Antonio Spurs that chronicles the history and accomplishments of the team.
Includes access to the Team Spirit website which provides additional
information and photos"-- Provided by publisher.
  ISBN 978-1-59953-641-5 (library edition : alk. paper) -- ISBN
978-1-60357-650-5 (ebook)
  1. San Antonio Spurs (Basketball team)--History--Juvenile literature. I.
Title.
  GV885.52.S26S84 2014
  796.323'6409764351--dc23
                                          2014006941

253N—072014
Manufactured in the United States of America in North Mankato, Minnesota.

COVER PHOTO: The Spurs are one of basketball's hardest working teams,
but they know how to have fun, too.

Table of Contents

ABOUT OUR GLOSSARY

In this book, there may be several words that you are reading for the first time. Some are sports words, some are new vocabulary words, and some are familiar words that are used in an unusual way. All of these words are defined on page 46. Throughout the book, sports words appear in **bold type**. Regular vocabulary words appear in ***bold italic type***.

Meet the Spurs

Basketball demands great individual talent, but the sport also rewards unselfish team play. The San Antonio Spurs are proof of this. The Spurs have had some of the game's most outrageously skilled players. Yet only when they blended their talents did they become champions.

What makes the Spurs a little different? Their players often come from a wide range of backgrounds. The same is true of San Antonio's coaches. When they all work together, the result is fantastic.

This book tells the story of the Spurs. From its earliest days, the team was famous for having fun on the court and playing entertaining basketball. Fans never knew when something might happen that they'd never seen before. And win or lose, they always left a Spurs game with something to talk about.

Coach Gregg Popovich gives instructions to Tony Parker. They helped the Spurs win three championships in a five-year span.

Glory Days

During the 1960s, Texas went crazy for **professional** sports. Early in the *decade*, the state fielded three pro football teams and a major league baseball team. In 1967, Texas got its first pro basketball team, the Dallas Chaparrals. A chaparral is a bird common to the Southwest. The Chaparrals (or Chaps, for short) were part of the **American Basketball Association (ABA)**, a new league that played its first season in 1967–68.

The ABA featured high-scoring games that showcased the talents of players who were overlooked by the older **National Basketball Association (NBA)**. The Chaparrals were one of the better teams in the early years of the ABA. Their stars included John Beasley, Glen Combs, Cincy Powell, Rich Jones, Steve Jones, Ron Boone, and Donnie Freeman. They made the **playoffs** in each of their first five seasons.

Despite their success, the Chaps failed to catch on with Dallas fans. The team was in danger of folding when a group of investors bought the club in 1973. The new owners moved the Chaps to San Antonio, and renamed them the Spurs. Fans in San Antonio had never had their own professional team—in any sport. The city fell in love with the Spurs and their wide-open style of basketball.

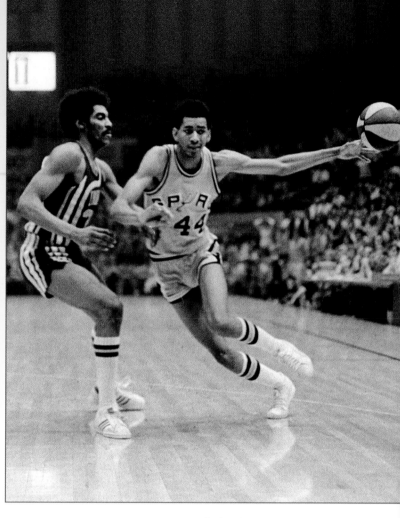

The first star to wear the Spurs uniform was George Gervin. He was a graceful player who could put the ball in the basket a dozen different ways. Along with James Silas and Larry Kenon, Gervin turned the Spurs into one of the highest scoring teams in history. San Antontio won a lot of games, and attracted a lot of fans.

LEFT: This old ABA uniform patch shows a chaparral.
ABOVE: George Gervin makes a move to the basket.

In 1976, the Spurs were one of four ABA teams invited to join the NBA. In their second season, they won the **Central Division**, and Gervin was the NBA's top scorer. During the 1980s, he was joined by Johnny Moore, Mike Mitchell, and Artis Gilmore. The Spurs reached the finals of the **Western Conference** twice. Both times they were defeated by the Los Angeles Lakers.

In 1989, a talented center named David Robinson joined the team. San Antonio added more good players in the years that followed. However, in 1996–97, Robinson missed most of the year with an injury and the Spurs finished in last place. The silver lining was that they wound up with the first pick in the **draft**. They selected another *agile* big man, Tim Duncan. In 1998–99, Duncan and Robinson led a talented squad that included Sean Elliott, Avery Johnson, and Mario Elie. They reached the **NBA Finals** for the first time and defeated the New York Knicks for their first championship.

LEFT: David Robinson helped turn the Spurs into the NBA's best team.
ABOVE: Tim Duncan celebrates a San Antonio championship.

Five years later, in Robinson's final season, the Spurs returned to the NBA Finals and won again. Duncan was now the leader on the floor. He got help from young guards Tony Parker and Stephen Jackson, and forwards Manu Ginobili and Bruce Bowen.

San Antonio won it all again in 2005 and 2007. These teams were built around Duncan, Parker, and Ginobili. All three players were born outside the Unites States. Never before had a championship team relied on a core of foreign players.

Over the years, this would become San Antonio's calling card. The team welcomed more stars from overseas, including Fabricio Oberto,

Ime Udoka, Tiago Splitter, Boris Diaw, and Marco Belinelli. No matter where a player was born, he felt at home in the San Antonio locker room. And Spurs fans made these *international* stars feel just as welcome on the court.

In 2012–13, Duncan, Parker, and Ginobili led the team back to the NBA Finals. The Spurs battled the Miami Heat for seven *grueling* games. They held the lead heading into the last few minutes of the decisive contest, but Miami stormed back for the victory. Even in defeat, the Spurs showed the kind of heart and class that have made them champions to their fans. Dreams of the San Antonio's next NBA title began immediately.

LEFT: Manu Ginobili glides to the hoop for a layup.
ABOVE: Like Ginobili, Tony Parker was one of several international stars who made the Spurs a powerhouse.

Home Court

T he Spurs have had three homes since moving to San Antonio in 1973. They played in the HemisFair Arena for 20 years. Next, the team moved to the Alamodome, which hosted many large-scale events, including football games. It could hold more than 30,000 fans for basketball games.

In 2002, the Spurs moved into a new arena built specially for basketball. It was designed to fit in with the city's history and natural beauty. The park surrounding the arena reminds fans of the state's breathtaking landscape.

BY THE NUMBERS

- The Spurs' arena has 18,581 seats for basketball.

- An art collection on view in the arena is worth more than $1 million.

- As of 2014, the Spurs had retired seven uniform numbers—6 (Avery Johnson), 12 (Bruce Bowen), 13 (James Silas), 32 (Sean Elliott), 44 (George Gervin), 50 (David Robinson), and 00 (Johnny Moore).

The Spurs take on the Los Angeles Lakers on San Antonio's home court. The team's championship banners can be seen hanging from the rafters.

Dressed for Success

W hen the team was known as the Chaparrals, its colors were red, white, and blue. After the move to San Antonio, the Spurs took the court for **preseason** games in the same colors. But on opening night in 1973, fans were amazed to see the players in cool silver-white-and-black uniforms. The new team *logo* made the U in SPURS look like the spur on the bottom of a cowboy boot. San Antonio has used the same style ever since.

The Spurs were one of the first teams to use black as a primary uniform color. Now black and silver are very popular colors in all pro sports. This has made Spurs uniforms and souvenirs best-selling items among basketball fans.

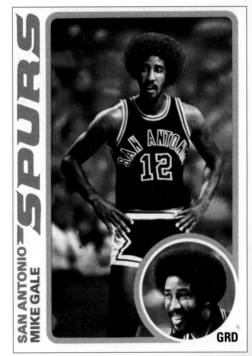

SAN ANTONIO
MIKE GALE
SPURS
12
GRD

LEFT: Marco Belinelli wears the team's 2013–14 home uniform.
ABOVE: Mike Gale models the Spurs' black-and-silver road uniform of the 1970s.

When the Spurs joined the NBA in 1976, they quickly became one of the most exciting teams in the league. Unfortunately, their high-scoring style did not translate into a championship. San Antonio took a step in that direction in 1996, when the team hired a little-known coach named Gregg Popovich. A year later, college star Tim Duncan joined the team. He combined with David Robinson to give the Spurs a dynamic duo along the front line.

Popovich coached his team to play tough defense. Robinson and Duncan led the way. In 1999, the Spurs reached the NBA Finals for the first time. They beat the New York Knicks to capture the championship. Duncan was named the **Most Valuable Player (MVP)** of the series.

Heading into the 2002–03 season, Robinson decided he was ready to retire. His teammates wanted to give him a "going away" present. The Spurs raced through the playoffs and met the New Jersey Nets in the NBA Finals. San Antonio would not be denied. The Spurs won the championship in six games. Duncan was named MVP once again, and Robinson celebrated like he was a little kid.

Two years later, the Spurs claimed their first NBA title without Robinson. Duncan led a lineup of international stars, including Tony Parker of

LEFT: David Robinson and Tim Duncan celebrate San Antonio's first title.
ABOVE: Tony Parker shows the fans which team is #1.

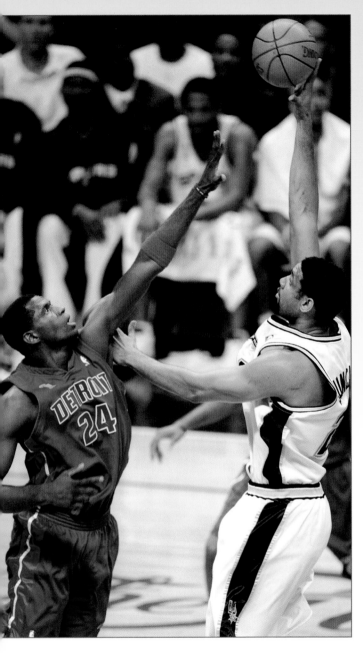

Belgium and Manu Ginobili of Argentina, into the NBA Finals against the Detroit Pistons.

The teams entered Game 5 tied at two games each. San Antonio won in **overtime**, but the Pistons fought back in Game 6 to knot the series again. Game 7 went back and forth until Duncan took over and gave the Spurs the lead for good. When the final buzzer sounded, they had their third championship in seven seasons.

In 2007, the Spurs won their fourth title. Their lineup hadn't changed much—the only new starter was **veteran** Michael Finley. During the playoffs that year, Finley set a team record with eight **3-pointers** in a game. The Spurs were never really in trouble during the **postseason**. They lost only four games on their way to the NBA Finals.

San Antonio faced LeBron James and the Cleveland Cavaliers for the championship. The Spurs had an edge in experience and used it to their advantage. They won the first two games easily. They also took Game 3, earning a 75–72 victory in a tough defensive battle. It was the lowest-scoring contest in the NBA Finals since 1955. Cleveland had a lead in Game 4, but San Antonio went on a 12–3 run and held on to win for the sweep.

In the locker room after the game, the Spurs rejoiced. Although Tony Parker was named MVP of the series, it was a true team victory. San Antonio made the right plays at key moments in each of the four games thanks to veterans like Finley. Finley was in his 12th NBA season, but this was his first championship. He could hardly believe it when his teammates handed him the game ball. That's what it means to be a Spur.

LEFT: Tim Duncan rises for a shot in the fourth quarter of Game 7 against the Pistons. **ABOVE**: Michael Finley holds up the game ball after San Antonio's 2007 championship.

To be a true star in the NBA, you need more than a great shot. You have to be a "go-to guy"—someone teammates trust to make the winning play when the seconds are ticking away in a big game. Spurs fans have had a lot to cheer about over the years, including these great stars …

THE PIONEERS

JAMES SILAS   6′ 2″ Guard

• BORN: 2/11/1949 • PLAYED FOR TEAM: 1972–73 TO 1980–81

James Silas ran the team's offense in the 1970s. He was a good passer and shooter, and a great *clutch* player. The fans called him "Captain Late" because he was at his best at the end of close games.

GEORGE GERVIN   6′ 7″ Guard

• BORN: 4/27/1952 • PLAYED FOR TEAM: 1974–75 TO 1984–85

George Gervin was nicknamed "Iceman" because no one was cooler under pressure. He averaged more than 20 points a game 12 years in a row. Gervin's favorite move was the finger-roll. He would rise to the basket with the ball cupped in one hand, and then flick it over defenders and into the basket.

LARRY KENON   6′ 9″ Forward

- BORN: 12/13/1952   • PLAYED FOR TEAM: 1976–77 TO 1979–80

Larry Kenon was a great rebounder and scorer. No one was better at finishing a fast break. His nickname was "Special K" for his high-flying moves.

BILLY PAULTZ   6′ 11″ Center

- BORN: 7/30/1948   • PLAYED FOR TEAM: 1976–77 TO 1979–80 & 1982–83

Billy Paultz was known as the "Whopper." He could shoot from the outside, glide into the lane for a hook shot, or use his wide body to get shots close to the hoop.

MIKE MITCHELL   6′ 7″ Forward

- BORN: 1/1/1956   • DIED: 6/9/2011   • PLAYED FOR TEAM: 1981–82 TO 1986–87

During the 1980s, Mike Mitchell teamed with George Gervin to give the Spurs an awesome scoring punch. He kept teammates loose with his deep laugh. He burned opponents with his accurate jump shot.

ALVIN ROBERTSON   6′ 3″ Guard

- BORN: 7/22/1962
- PLAYED FOR TEAM: 1984–85 TO 1988–89

Alvin Robertson was the best defensive guard in team history. He led the NBA in steals twice for San Antonio. Robertson was named Defensive Player of the Year in 1985–86, when he set a record with 301 steals.

RIGHT: Alvin Robertson

DAVID ROBINSON 7′ 1″ Center

- BORN: 8/6/1965
- PLAYED FOR TEAM: 1989–90 TO 2002–03

The Spurs drafted David Robinson in 1987, and then waited for two years while he served his country in the Navy. The "Admiral" was worth it. Robinson won the NBA scoring title in 1993–94 and the MVP in 1994–95.

SEAN ELLIOTT 6′ 8″ Forward

- BORN: 2/2/1968
- PLAYED FOR TEAM: 1990–91 TO 1993–94
  & 1995–96 TO 2000–01

Sean Elliott was a smooth, confident shooter. He loved to take—and *make*—shots at the buzzer. His most famous was a 3-pointer to beat the Portland Trailblazers in the 1999 playoffs. San Antonio fans still call it the "Memorial Day Miracle."

TIM DUNCAN 7′ 0″ Forward

- BORN: 4/25/1976 • FIRST SEASON WITH TEAM: 1997–98

Tim Duncan wanted to be a world champion swimmer when he was growing up. Instead, he became the leader of four championship teams for the Spurs. Duncan was a fierce competitor with a light shooting touch. He was named NBA MVP twice.

ABOVE: David Robinson and Tim Duncan work together to defend Kobe Bryant of the Los Angeles Lakers. **RIGHT**: Manu Ginobili

BRUCE BOWEN

6′ 7″ Forward

- BORN: 6/14/1971   • PLAYED FOR TEAM: 2001–02 TO 2008–09

No forward in the NBA played tougher defense than Bruce Bowen. He was named to the league's **All-Defensive Team** every season he played for San Antonio. Although Bowen never averaged double-figures in scoring, the Spurs retired his number in 2012.

TONY PARKER

6′ 2″ Guard

- BORN: 5/17/1982   • FIRST SEASON WITH TEAM: 2001–02

Tony Parker was born in Belgium and grew up in France. The Spurs discovered him when he was 18. Parker had incredible speed and an unstoppable "tear drop" shot. He was voted MVP of the 2007 NBA Finals.

MANU GINOBILI   6′ 6″ Guard

- BORN: 7/28/1977
- FIRST SEASON WITH TEAM: 2002–03

Manu Ginobili was a star in Argentina before joining the Spurs. His desire to win rubbed off on all his teammates. Ginobili was equally good as a starter or a **sixth man**. Few players were better at changing the pace of a game.

MANU GINOBILI
Guard • San Antonio Spurs

Calling the Shots

When the team started as the Chaparrals, it made headlines with its first coach. Cliff Hagan was a tough leader who had been an **All-Star** in the NBA. He worked his players very hard, and the Chaps rewarded him with plenty of big victories.

After the Spurs joined the NBA in 1976, Doug Moe became their coach. Moe had been an All-Star in the ABA. He borrowed from the league's exciting style and created a "run-and-gun" offense that made San Antonio one of the most popular teams in basketball.

Stan Albeck was another successful coach for San Antonio. He led the Spurs to the **Western Conference Finals** twice in three seasons during the early 1980s. Later in the decade, Larry Brown called the shots in San Antonio. He demanded maximum effort and unselfish play from everyone on the team. Under Brown, the Spurs won two **Midwest Division** titles.

Gregg Popovich proved to be the best fit for the Spurs. He had spent many years as an assistant coach, including several seasons with San Antonio. When Peter Holt bought the Spurs in

The Spurs didn't become a championship team until Gregg Popovich became the head coach.

1993, he hired Popovich to handle the club's business. In 1996–97, after the Spurs got off to a slow start, Popovich took on the coaching job himself. Two years later, the Spurs were NBA champions.

Popovich led the Spurs to three more championships, in 2003, 2005, and 2007. San Antonio went to the Western Conference Finals three more times after that, and returned to the NBA Finals in 2013. As of the 2013–14 season, Popovich was the longest-serving coach in the four major team sports—basketball, baseball, football, and hockey.

One Great Day

Even though the Spurs won their first NBA championship in 1999, they didn't feel completely satisfied. Their title came at the end of a shortened season. A disagreement between team owners and players had trimmed the schedule to 50 games. To many fans, this cast a shadow over San Antonio's first NBA crown.

The Spurs immediately set their sights on winning another championship. By 2002–03, they were in position again to make a run at the league title. No team in the NBA won more games, and no team was playing better as the playoffs began. San Antonio beat the Phoenix Suns, Los Angeles Lakers, and Dallas Mavericks to reach the NBA Finals. The Spurs faced the New Jersey Nets for the championship.

After five exhausting games, the Spurs held a one-game lead. They needed just one more victory, but it would not be easy. The

David Robinson went out a winner after San Antonio's 2003 NBA title.

two teams battled hard in Game 6. The Nets led by six points in the fourth quarter. Gregg Popovich called a timeout. The Spurs knew it was time to dig down and find something extra.

The Spurs increased their intensity on defense and made tough baskets when they needed them. They capped their great comeback with an 88–77 victory. San Antonio had earned its second championship, and no one could question this one. It was all the more special because David Robinson had announced his retirement. The Admiral left a champion, with 13 points and 17 rebounds in his final game.

Legend Has It

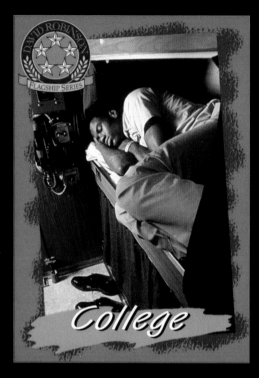

College

Which Spur traded a career underwater for a career on the court?

LEGEND HAS IT that David Robinson did. As a teenager, Robinson dreamed of being the captain of a submarine. He was thrilled to be accepted by the U.S. Naval Academy in 1983. Robinson stood 6'2" at the time. He grew nine inches in college—so big that he could not fit into the cramped space of a submarine. Although Robinson's nickname was the Admiral, the highest rank he achieved in the Navy was lieutenant.

ABOVE: This trading card shows how difficult it was for David Robinson to fit in his submarine bunk after his growth spurt.

...ho was the first Spur to have a ...n club?

LEGEND HAS IT that Swen Nater was. Nater played just one full season for the Spurs, in 1974–75. He was a very nice guy who was friendly with the San Antonio fans. A group calling itself "Nater's Raiders" began showing up at games to cheer for their hero. With his fan club rooting him on, Nater led the league in rebounding that year.

...d Hurricane Hugo help the Spurs ...ecome NBA champions?

LEGEND HAS IT that it did. At the time of the storm in 1989, Tim Duncan was 13 years old and one of the top young freestyle swimmers in the world. Hugo slammed into his home country of St. Croix, and destroyed every swimming pool on the island. Duncan soon started playing basketball with his brother-in-law, who was a basketball coach. The rest, as they say, is history!

Can one play make or break a championship season? Many Spurs fans think so. As proof, they point to Game 2 of the 1999 Western Conference Finals, with San Antonio facing the Portland Trailblazers. The contest was played on the Monday of Memorial Day weekend. The Trailblazers led by 18 points in the third quarter. The game looked like it was over—until the Spurs found their rhythm.

San Antonio tightened its defense and closed the gap. The Spurs trailed by a point with time running out. They fouled Damon Stoudamire with 12 seconds left. He made one of two free throws to give Portland an 85–83 lead. Gregg Popovich called timeout and looked at his team. Instead of asking David Robinson or Tim Duncan to attempt the game-tying shot, he called a play for forward Sean Elliott.

If the doctors had had their way, Elliott would not even have been on the court. He was suffering from a serious kidney ailment. In ten weeks, he would undergo a transplant operation. However,

Sean Elliott goes strong to the hoop against Portland in Game 2 of the 1999 Western Conference Finals.

anyone who knew Elliott knew there was no way he was going to miss the playoffs.

As Elliott took the in-bounds pass from Mario Elie, the only thing on his mind was getting a good look at the basket. He was so focused that he nearly stepped on the sideline. With Portland center Rasheed Wallace rushing toward him, Elliott dribbled once, turned, and let fly a fall-away jump shot. The ball barely cleared Wallace's fingertips and fell through the hoop for Elliott's sixth 3-pointer of the game.

Elliott's desperate basket gave the Spurs their only lead of the day. They held on for an 86–85 victory. San Antonio went on to sweep the Trailblazers, and then defeated the New York Knicks in the NBA Finals. To this day, fans still talk about Elliott's "Memorial Day Miracle."

Team Spirit

Fans in San Antonio are thankful to have the Spurs. The city worked hard to get an NBA team. The fans have become very knowledgeable about basketball. They are also very noisy. This gives the Spurs a great home court advantage.

One of basketball's most famous fan groups roots for the Spurs. They call themselves the "Baseline Bums." They have been around since the 1970s, when they were led by "Big George" and "Dancing Harry." The Baseline Bums are hard to miss— they sit right above the tunnel that leads to the locker rooms. They are fiercely proud of their team and their city, and they aren't afraid to let visiting teams know it.

MIKE MITCHELL TRIBUTE NIGHT
JANUARY 4, 2012
SPURS SPORTS

LEFT: Tim Duncan celebrates with fans after a San Antonio championship.
ABOVE: The Spurs often hold special events honoring past stars such as Mike Mitchell. Mitchell passed away in 2011.

The basketball season is played from October through June. That means each season takes place at the end of one year and the beginning of the next. In this timeline, the accomplishments of the Chaps and Spurs are shown by season.

1973–74
The team moves to San Antonio.

1981–82
George Gervin wins his fourth NBA scoring title.

1967–68
The Chaps join the ABA.

1976–77
The Spurs join the NBA.

1989–90
David Robinson is named **Rookie of the Year**.

Rich Jones was a star for the Chaps.

RICH JONES
CHAPARRALS' FORWARD

David Robinson poses in front of the Alamo in San Antonio on this magazine cover.

Kawhi
Leonard

1998–99
The Spurs win
their first NBA
championship.

2002–03
The Spurs win
their second NBA
championship.

2011–12
Kawhi Leonard
is named to the
All-Rookie Team.

2001–02
Tim Duncan is
named MVP.

2006–07
The Spurs win their fourth
NBA championship.

2012–13
The Spurs win their
fifth conference title.

Tim Duncan, Tony
Parker, and Manu
Ginobili became
the core of the team
starting in 2002–03.

Fun Facts

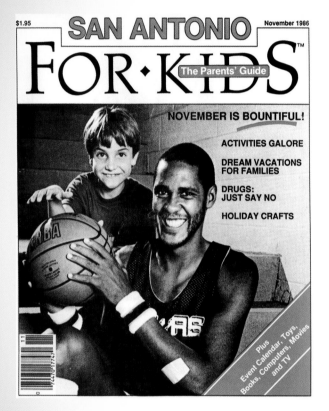

$1.95 • SAN ANTONIO • November 1986

FOR·KIDS™
The Parents' Guide

NOVEMBER IS BOUNTIFUL!

ACTIVITIES GALORE

DREAM VACATIONS FOR FAMILIES

DRUGS: JUST SAY NO

HOLIDAY CRAFTS

Plus Event Calendar, Toys, Books, Computers, Movies and TV

20-20-20

During the 1980s, the Spurs' top playmaker was guard Johnny Moore. He led the team to the conference finals twice and had three games of 20 **assists** in his career.

MAN OF STEAL

In a 1976–77 game, Larry Kenon had 29 points, 15 rebounds, and 11 steals. His steals total set an NBA record. It took 23 years before another player matched it.

FOUR ON THE FLOOR

In a 1985–86 game, Alvin Robertson scored 20 points and added 11 rebounds, 10 assists, and 10 steals. He became the first NBA player to complete a **quadruple-double** with 10 or more steals.

RAISE THE ROOF

When the Spurs moved into the HemisFair Arena in 1973, it held about 10,000 fans. After George Gervin joined the team, demand for tickets soared. The Spurs decided to raise the roof on the arena so that 6,000 more seats could be added.

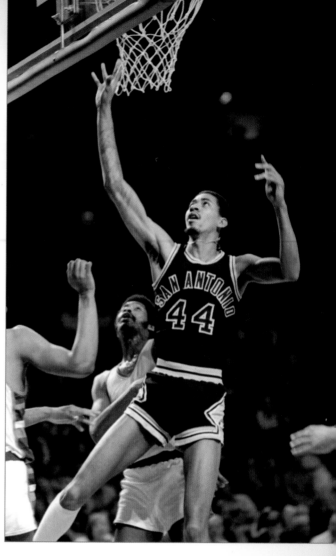

GOLDEN BOY

After his second season with the Spurs, Manu Ginobili led Argentina's basketball team to victories over the United States and Spain to win a gold medal at the 2004 *Olympics*. It was the first gold medal for Ginobili's home country in any sport since 1952.

BLACK AND BLUE

In the 1980s, San Antonio's front line featured some of the roughest players in the NBA, including Artis Gilmore, George Johnson, Dave Corzine, and Mark Olberding. Fans called them the "Bruise Brothers."

LEFT: Like many Spurs, Johnny Moore got involved with kids in the community.   **ABOVE**: George Gervin scores two of the 23,602 points he recorded for San Antonio.

Talking Basketball

SPURS

JAMES SILAS • G

"You don't take the shot that people give you. You take the shot that you want. I was good at being able to go where I wanted to go on the floor and take the shot that I wanted, not the shot that the defensive player expected me to take."

▶ **James Silas,** *on taking a shot with the game on the line*

"I watched Julius Erving, Wilt Chamberlain, and Connie Hawkins. I watched those three greats use the finger-roll, and I kind of copied them. And I'm the one who became famous for it."

▶ **George Gervin,** *on his favorite shot*

"No question he's the greatest power forward ever. It's hard to compare anyone to Tim. He's in a class by himself."

▶ **David Robinson,** *on Tim Duncan*

"He's aggressive and he has no fear."

▶ **Gregg Popovich,**
on Tony Parker

"To me, defense is a mental attitude … it takes will and heart to go out there and lock your man up."

▶ **Michael Finley,** *on the secret to playing great defense*

"This is the biggest thing to ever happen in San Antonio!"

▶ **Avery Johnson,** *on the Spurs' 1999 championship*

"He puts his head down and he goes, and we pray for the best."

▶ **Tim Duncan,** *on the aggressive style of Manu Ginobili*

LEFT: James Silas   **ABOVE**: Gregg Popovich and Tony Parker

Great Debates

People who root for the Spurs love to compare their favorite moments, teams, and players. Some debates have been going on for years! How would you settle these classic basketball arguments?

Manu Ginobili is the Spurs' all-time best long-distance shooter ...

... because his ability to hit 3-pointers helped the team win three championships. With Tony Parker and Tim Duncan attacking the basket, San Antonio's opponents were tempted to protect the rim on defense. That often left Ginobili (LEFT) open at the 3-point line. For his career, he hit on almost 40 percent of those shots.

No way! Chuck Person could outshoot Ginobili any day of the week...

... because 3-pointers were his specialty. Long before Person joined the Spurs in 1994–95, he was a long-distance shooting legend. When he arrived in San Antonio, he was still a great marksman. In his first season with the Spurs, Person started only one game, but he led the team in 3-pointers with 172. The following season, he set a team record with 190.

.. because it set a San Antonio record and earned him the NBA scoring crown. Robinson (**RIGHT**) needed a huge game against the Los Angeles Clippers on the final day of the 1993–94 season to pass Shaquille O'Neal for the league scoring title. Robinson made 26 of 41 shots (including a 3-pointer) and hit 18 of 25 free throws. His 71 points enabled him to barely edge O'Neal.

Not so fast. George Gervin's 63-point game in 1977-78 was far more impressive . . .

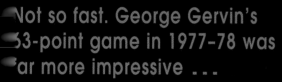

.. because he had to earn every point. While Robinson scored on layups, dunks, and short jumpers, the Iceman got his points on twisting drives, graceful finger-rolls, and smooth jump shots. In 1977–78, Gervin needed 60 points to beat David Thompson of the Denver Nuggets in the closest scoring race in league history. Gervin was unstoppable in the first half with 53 points. He added 10 more after halftime and became the first Spur to ever lead the NBA in scoring.

For the Record

T he great Chaps and Spurs teams and players have left their marks on the record books. These are the "best of the best" …

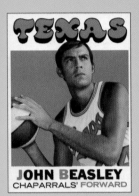

John Beasley

George Gervin

SPURS AWARD WINNERS

ABA ALL-STAR GAME MVP
John Beasley	1968–69

ABA ROOKIE OF THE YEAR
Swen Nater	1973–74

NBA COACH OF THE YEAR
Gregg Popovich	2002–03
Gregg Popovich	2011–12

NBA FINALS MVP
Tim Duncan	1998–99
Tim Duncan	2002–03
Tim Duncan	2004–05
Tony Parker	2006–07

NBA ALL-STAR GAME MVP
George Gervin	1979–80

NBA DEFENSIVE PLAYER OF THE YEAR
David Robinson	1991–92

NBA SIXTH MAN AWARD
Manu Ginobili	2007–08

NBA 3-POINT SHOOTOUT CHAMPION
Marco Belinelli	2013–14

NBA ROOKIE OF THE YEAR
David Robinson	1989–90
Tim Duncan	1997–98

NBA MVP
David Robinson	1994–95
Tim Duncan	2001–02
Tim Duncan	2002–03

SPURS ACHIEVEMENTS

ACHIEVEMENT	SEASON
Central Division Champions	1977–78
Central Division Champions	1978–79
Midwest Division Champions	1980–81
Midwest Division Champions	1981–82
Midwest Division Champions	1982–83
Midwest Division Champions	1989–90
Midwest Division Champions	1990–91
Midwest Division Champions	1994–95
Midwest Division Champions	1995–96
Midwest Division Champions	1998–99
NBA Champions	1998–99
Midwest Division Champions	2000–01
Midwest Division Champions	2001–02
Midwest Division Champions	2002–03
NBA Champions	2002–03
Midwest Division Champions	2004–05
NBA Champions	2004–05
NBA Champions	2006–07
Southwest Division Champions	2008–09
Southwest Division Champions	2010–11
Southwest Division Champions	2011–12
Southwest Division Champions	2012–13
Western Conference Champions	2012–13
Southwest Division Champions	2013–14

ABOVE: Tim Duncan shares his 2002 MVP trophy with San Antonio fans.
LEFT: Artis Gilmore gets ready to go up for a shot. He starred for the Spurs in the 1980s.

Pinpoints

The history of a basketball team is made up of many smaller stories. These stories take place all over the map—not just in the city a team calls "home." Match the pushpins on these maps to the **TEAM FACTS**, and you will begin to see the story of the Chaps and Spurs unfold!

TEAM FACTS

1 Dallas, Texas—*The team played here as the Chaps from 1967 to 1973.*

2 San Antonio, Texas—*The team has played here since 1973.*

3 Tucson, Arizona—*Sean Elliott was born here.*

4 Tallulah, Louisiana—*James Silas was born here.*

5 Birmingham, Alabama—*Larry Kenon was born here.*

6 Manassas, Virginia—*David Robinson was born here.*

7 East Chicago, Indiana—*Gregg Popovich was born here.*

8 Detroit, Michigan—*George Gervin was born here.*

9 St. Croix, U.S. Virgin Islands—*Tim Duncan was born here.*

10 San Giovanni in Perciseto, Italy—*Marco Belinelli was born here.*

11 Bruges, Belgium—*Tony Parker was born here.*

12 Bahia Blanca, Argentina—*Manu Ginobili was born here.*

Larry Kenon

Glossary

🏀 Basketball Words
🧠 Vocabulary Words

3-POINTERS—Baskets made from behind the 3-point line.

AGILE—Quick and graceful.

ALL-DEFENSIVE TEAM—The annual honor given to the NBA's best defensive players at each position.

ALL-ROOKIE TEAM—The annual honor given to the NBA's best first-year players at each position.

ALL-STAR—A player selected to play in the annual All-Star Game.

AMERICAN BASKETBALL ASSOCIATION (ABA)—The basketball league that played for nine seasons starting in 1967. Prior to the 1976–77 season, four ABA teams joined the NBA, and the rest went out of business.

ASSISTS—Passes that lead to baskets.

CENTRAL DIVISION—A group of teams that plays in the central part of the country.

CLUTCH—Able to perform well under pressure.

DECADE—A period of 10 years; also specific periods, such as the 1950s.

DRAFT—The annual meeting during which NBA teams choose from a group of the best college and foreign players.

GRUELING—Exhausting.

INTERNATIONAL—From all over the world.

LOGO—A symbol or design that represents a company or team.

MIDWEST DIVISION—A group of teams that plays in the central part of the country.

MOST VALUABLE PLAYER (MVP)—The annual award given to the league's best player; also given to the best player in the league finals and All-Star Game.

NATIONAL BASKETBALL ASSOCIATION (NBA)—The professional league that has been operating since 1946–47.

NBA FINALS—The playoff series that decides the champion of the league.

OLYMPICS—An international sports competition held every four years.

OVERTIME—The extra period played when a game is tied after 48 minutes.

PLAYOFFS—The games played after the season to determine the league champion.

POSTSEASON—Another term for playoffs.

PRESEASON—The practice games played before a season starts.

PROFESSIONAL—A player or team that plays a sport for money.

QUADRUPLE-DOUBLE—A game in which a player records double-figures in four different statistical categories.

ROOKIE OF THE YEAR—The annual award given to the league's best first-year player.

SIXTH MAN—The first player to come off the bench for a team.

VETERAN—A player with great experience.

WESTERN CONFERENCE—A group of teams that play in the West. The winner of the Western Conference meets the winner of the Eastern Conference in the league finals.

WESTERN CONFERENCE FINALS—The playoff series that determines which team from the West will play the best team in the East for the NBA championship.

FAST BREAK

TEAM SPIRIT introduces a great way to stay up to date with your team! Visit our **FAST BREAK** link and get connected to the latest and greatest updates. **FAST BREAK** serves as a young reader's ticket to an exclusive web page—with more stories, fun facts, team records, and photos of the Spurs. Content is updated during and after each season. The **FAST BREAK** feature also enables readers to send comments and letters to the author! Log onto:

www.norwoodhousepress.com/library.aspx

and click on the tab: **TEAM SPIRIT** to access **FAST BREAK**.

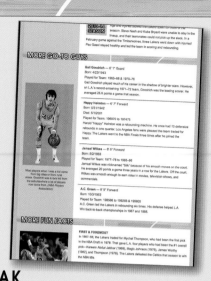

Read all the books in the series to learn more about professional sports. For a complete listing of the baseball, basketball, football, and hockey teams in the **TEAM SPIRIT** series, visit our website at:

www.norwoodhousepress.com/library.aspx

On the Road

SAN ANTONIO SPURS
One AT&T Center Parkway
San Antonio, Texas 78219
(210) 444-5000
www.Spurs.com

**NAISMITH MEMORIAL
BASKETBALL HALL OF FAME**
1000 West Columbus Avenue
Springfield, Massachusetts 01105
(877) 4HOOPLA
www.hoophall.com

On the Bookshelf

To learn more about the sport of basketball, look for these books at your library or bookstore:

- Doeden, Matt. *Basketball Legends In the Making*. North Mankato, Minnesota: Capstone Press, 2014.

- Rappaport, Ken. *Basketball's Top 10 Slam Dunkers*. Berkeley Heights, New Jersey: Enslow Publishers, 2013.

- Silverman, Drew. *The NBA Finals*. Minneapolis, Minnesota: ABDO Group, 2013.

Index

PAGE NUMBERS IN **BOLD** REFER TO ILLUSTRATIONS.

THE TEAM

MARK STEWART has written more than 40 books on basketball, and over 150 sports books for kids. He grew up in New York City during the 1960s rooting for the Knicks and Nets, and was lucky enough to meet many of the stars of those teams. Mark comes from a family of writers. His grandfather was Sunday Editor of *The New York Times* and his mother was Articles Editor of *The Ladies' Home Journal* and *McCall's*. Mark has profiled hundreds of athletes over the last 20 years. He has also written several books about his native New York, and New Jersey, his home today. Mark is a graduate of Duke University, with a degree in History. He lives with his daughters and wife Sarah overlooking Sandy Hook, New Jersey.